Table Contents

Chapter 1: The Visionary Blueprint

1-Introduction to Paul Biya's early vision for Cameroon's economic development.

1-1 Examination of key speeches and policy outlines that set the groundwork for his economic agenda.

1-2 Overview of the historical and global context that influenced Biya's vision.

Chapter 2: Economic Reforms and Modernization

2-1 Analysis of the economic reforms implemented by Biya during his leadership.

2-2 Exploration of policies aimed at modernizing key sectors, including finance, industry, and agriculture.

2-3 Examination of the role of economic diversification in reducing dependency on specific industries.

Chapter 3: Infrastructure Revolution

3-1 In-depth look at major infrastructure projects initiated under Biya's administration, including roads, bridges, energy, and telecommunications.

3-2 Evaluation of the impact of these projects on regional connectivity, trade, and overall economic development.

Chapter 4: Social Development Programs

4-1 Overview of social welfare programs implemented to improve healthcare, education, and poverty alleviation.

4-2 Case studies and success stories highlighting the impact of these programs on the lives of the Cameroonian people.

Chapter 5: Foreign Relations and Economic Diplomacy

5-1 Exploration of Biya's strategies for attracting foreign investment and fostering economic partnerships.

5-2 Analysis of trade policies and international collaborations that contributed to Cameroon's economic growth.

5-3 Examination of challenges faced in navigating the global economic landscape.

Chapter 6: Challenges and Controversies in Economic Management

6-1 Candid discussion of economic challenges faced by Biya's administration.

6-2 Examination of controversies, including corruption allegations, and their impact on economic development.

6-3 Analysis of adaptive measures taken in response to economic crises.

Chapter 7: Sustainable Development and Environmental Policies

7-1 Exploration of initiatives aimed at balancing economic development with environmental sustainability.

7-2 Case studies on conservation efforts and policies addressing the environmental impact of economic activities.

Chapter 8: Legacy and Continuity

8-1 Reflection on Paul Biya's lasting impact on Cameroon's economy.

8-2 Evaluation of the legacy left in terms of economic stability, growth, and social development.

8-3 Analysis of how subsequent leaders built upon or diverged from Biya's economic initiatives.

Conclusion: Cameroon's Economic Trajectory

8- 4 Synthesis of key findings from each chapter.

8- 5 Reflection on the overall trajectory of Cameroon's economic development under Paul Biya's leadership.

8-6 Consideration of future challenges and opportunities for sustained economic growth in Cameroon.

Biyasites and the African Revolution: Certainly, here's a detailed breakdown of the chapters and their content for a book focusing on Paul Biya's development and economic initiatives in Cameroon: and some of the remarkable western friends that he held for some many years.

Chapter 1: The Visionary Blueprint

Introduction to Paul Biya's early vision for Cameroon's economic development.

Economic Reforms and Modernization

In the quest for economic prosperity, President Paul Biya embarked on a comprehensive journey of economic reforms and modernization, aiming to reshape Cameroon's financial landscape. This chapter examines the multifaceted approach to modernizing key sectors, with a particular focus on the struggles and triumphs faced by the youth. Recognizing the youth as a critical demographic, Biya's administration implemented programs and policies to harness their potential as engines of economic growth. Initiatives such as skill development, entrepreneurship programs, and educational reforms are explored in depth, shedding light on their impact on empowering the youth economically.

The struggle of the youth, however, was not limited to economic challenges alone. The chapter delves into the intersectionality of economic struggles and the military landscape, addressing how the youth, often faced with limited economic opportunities, may be drawn into military activities. It examines the complexities of this relationship, including the role of the military in providing stability for economic development and the potential for youth involvement in both constructive economic endeavors and military activities. Through this exploration, we gain insights into the delicate balance required to ensure that economic development positively influences the lives of the youth and contributes to the nation's overall prosperity without compromising its security.

SESSION 1: The Visionary Blueprint: Igniting the Hope of the Youth

In the inaugural chapter, we explore President Paul Biya's visionary blueprint for Cameroon, and how it resonates with the aspirations of the young African generation. Biya's vision goes beyond the traditional realms of politics and economics; it encompasses a profound understanding of the dreams and aspirations of the youth. This chapter delves into the mission and hope embedded in Biya's leadership, especially in the context of a continent where the youth are the vanguards of change and progress.

Within this visionary blueprint, the focus expands to the Cameroonian youth, who represent the future of not only their nation but the entire African continent. We examine Biya's commitment to providing a platform for the youth to articulate their visions, fostering an environment where their innovative ideas can contribute to the nation's self-care and economic recovery.

The chapter illuminates how Biya's administration envisioned self-care not only as an individual responsibility but as a collective effort to nurture the socio-economic fabric of the nation. By investing in education, healthcare, and social welfare programs tailored to the needs of the youth, Biya sought to instill a sense of responsibility and empowerment, turning them into active participants in the recovery and rebuilding of the Cameroonian economy.

Furthermore, we explore the concept of "mercy" as a guiding principle in the visionary blueprint, emphasizing the importance of compassion, understanding, and support in the journey toward economic recovery. This chapter highlights specific policies and initiatives designed to provide a safety net for those facing economic hardships, demonstrating how Biya's leadership aimed to create a compassionate society capable of lifting itself out of adversity.

As we navigate through the details of this visionary blueprint, the chapter also considers the long-term implications for the future of young Cameroonians and Africans at large. By fostering a climate of innovation, inclusivity, and resilience, Biya's vision lays the groundwork for a generation poised to lead the charge in redeveloping not just their nation but contributing significantly to the advancement of the entire African continent.

Examination of key speeches and policy outlines that set the groundwork for his economic agenda.

In understanding President Paul Biya's economic agenda for Cameroon, a thorough examination of his key speeches and policy outlines is essential. These pivotal moments not only reveal the intricacies of his vision but also provide insights into the foundational principles that shaped the nation's economic trajectory.

One of the seminal speeches that set the tone for Biya's economic vision occurred in [insert specific date or occasion]. In this address, the President articulated a comprehensive roadmap, emphasizing the significance of economic stability, diversification, and sustainable development. He highlighted the need for a strategic departure from dependency on a single sector and outlined a vision where Cameroon would harness its diverse resources for holistic growth.

Policy outlines accompanying these speeches further solidified Biya's economic agenda. Notable documents such as [insert policy names or references] served as guideposts for the implementation of key reforms. They addressed critical aspects like fiscal policy, trade regulations, and investment incentives. Biya's commitment to creating an enabling environment for business, both domestic and foreign, is evident in these documents, reflecting his belief in the private sector as a catalyst for economic development.

Moreover, the examination of these key speeches and policy outlines reveals President Biya's emphasis on human capital development. Education and skill enhancement emerged as cornerstones of his economic strategy, recognizing that a well-educated and skilled workforce is indispensable for sustainable growth. These documents unfolded initiatives aimed at nurturing talent, fostering innovation, and aligning education with the demands of a rapidly evolving global economy.

In summary, this chapter scrutinizes the rhetoric and policy architecture that laid the groundwork for Paul Biya's economic agenda. It traces the evolution of his economic vision, highlighting key moments where the President articulated his aspirations and the concrete policy measures he envisaged to propel Cameroon towards a more prosperous and self-sufficient future.

Overview of the historical and global context that influenced Biya's vision.

SESSION 2: Political Reforms and the Looming Shadow of Betrayal

As President Paul Biya undertook significant government reforms, introducing changes aimed at fostering efficiency and inclusivity, a complex tapestry of danger and opportunity unfolded. This chapter delves into the intricate dynamics surrounding these reforms, examining the palpable fear of power shifts among different ethnicities and communities.

- **The Danger of Overt Power Redistribution:**
    - Analysis of the apprehensions and resistance within government officials from historically dominant ethnicities as power dynamics shifted.
    - Exploration of the challenges faced in ensuring equitable representation without instigating resentment and opposition.
- **Opportunities in Inclusive Governance:**
    - Examination of the positive outcomes of embracing diversity in government, such as enriched policy perspectives and improved public trust.

- Case studies highlighting instances where inclusive governance contributed to national unity and collective progress.
- **The Peril of Betrayal and Internal Strife:**
    - Investigation into the seeds of discord sown within government circles due to the fear of betrayal.
    - Case studies on instances where political betrayals led to internal strife, disrupting governance and stability.
- **The Opportunistic Nature of Political Alliances:**
    - Exploration of how political alliances, formed out of necessity or convenience, presented opportunities for policy advancement.
    - Analysis of the delicate balance required to maintain alliances while safeguarding against opportunistic moves that could undermine the government.
- **The Traitor Within: Espionage and Internal Threats:**
    - Examination of internal threats posed by individuals within the government who exploited power shifts for personal gain.
    - Discussion on the measures taken to identify and counteract potential traitors, including enhanced security protocols and intelligence gathering.
- **The Challenge of Navigating Ethnic Tensions:**

- Analysis of the delicate task of addressing ethnic tensions without exacerbating divisions.
- Examination of policies and initiatives aimed at fostering national cohesion and shared identity.

This chapter uncovers the intricate interplay of danger and opportunity within the realm of political reforms, providing a nuanced understanding of the challenges faced by President Biya in steering the nation towards inclusive governance while mitigating the risks of betrayal and internal strife. Through a careful exploration of these dynamics, readers gain insight into the complexities of political power transitions and the enduring quest for stability in a diverse and evolving political landscape.

Chapter 2: Economic Reforms and Modernization

Introduction

Analysis of the economic reforms implemented by Biya during his leadership.

As of my last knowledge update in January 2022, Paul Biya has been in power in Cameroon since 1982. Economic reforms implemented by any leader should be analyzed within the context of the specific political, social, and economic conditions of the country. Biya's leadership in Cameroon has been marked by both positive and critical assessments of his economic policies. Please note that developments may have occurred since my last update.

Economic Reforms under Paul Biya:

Structural Adjustment Programs (SAP): In the 1980s and 1990s, Cameroon, like many African countries, implemented Structural Adjustment Programs in collaboration with the International Monetary Fund (IMF) and the World Bank. These programs aimed to stabilize the economy, reduce government intervention, and promote market-oriented policies. However, the SAPs faced criticism for their social impact, including austerity measures that affected vulnerable populations.

Diversification Efforts: There have been efforts to diversify the economy, reduce dependence on oil exports, and promote sectors like agriculture. However, the success of these efforts has been mixed, and challenges, including corruption and infrastructure deficiencies, have hindered progress.

Investment Promotion: Biya's government has aimed to attract foreign investment through various initiatives. While some projects have been successful, the overall investment climate in Cameroon has faced challenges, including bureaucratic hurdles and concerns about governance.

Challenges and Criticisms:

Corruption: Persistent issues of corruption have affected the effectiveness of economic reforms. Corruption can undermine the allocation of resources and hinder the intended impact of policies.

Income Inequality: Economic growth has not always translated into improved living standards for all Cameroonians. Income inequality remains a concern, with disparities between urban and rural areas.

Infrastructure Deficiencies: Inadequate infrastructure, including transportation and energy, has been identified as a hindrance to economic development. Insufficient infrastructure can limit the competitiveness of industries and impede growth.

Political Stability: The political stability of Cameroon has been both an asset and a concern. While stability can attract investment, it has also been associated with a long period of one-party rule and allegations of electoral irregularities.

Dynastic Concerns:

Paul Biya's long tenure has led to concerns about the emergence of a dynastic political system. The question of succession has been a topic of discussion, with Biya's prolonged rule raising issues related to democracy and the peaceful transition of power.

In conclusion, the economic reforms implemented under Paul Biya's leadership in Cameroon have been characterized by a mix of achievements and challenges. The success of these reforms depends on various factors, including the effectiveness of governance, the impact of global economic trends, and the ability to address underlying issues such as corruption and infrastructure deficiencies. The potential emergence of a dynastic political system adds another layer of complexity to the analysis of Cameroon's political and economic landscape.

Corruption and reformation, the conflict and the internal fight among leadership.

The interplay between corruption, internal conflicts, leadership struggles, and the influence of ethnicity and culture on power dynamics can significantly impact the governance and stability of a nation. Let's delve into the complexities of these interconnected issues:

Corruption:

Undermining Governance: Corruption erodes the foundations of good governance by diverting resources meant for public welfare to personal gain. It often flourishes when there's a lack of transparency, accountability, and effective anti-corruption measures.

Implications for Development: Rampant corruption inhibits economic development, impedes foreign investment, and exacerbates social inequalities. It hampers the efficient allocation of resources, hindering infrastructure and public service projects.

Reformation Efforts:

Legal and Institutional Overhaul: Effective reformation requires a comprehensive overhaul of legal and institutional frameworks. Strengthening anti-corruption laws, establishing independent oversight bodies, and ensuring swift and impartial judicial processes are crucial.

Cultural Shift: Successfully combating corruption often involves a cultural shift towards values of transparency, accountability, and integrity. Public awareness campaigns, education, and fostering a culture of ethical behavior can contribute to this shift.

Internal Conflicts and Leadership Struggles:

Power Struggles: Internal conflicts and leadership struggles often arise from competition for power, resources, or influence. These struggles can divert attention from addressing critical issues such as corruption and effective governance.

Ethnic and Cultural Dynamics: Internal conflicts may be fueled by ethnic or cultural divisions within the leadership. When power is perceived as favoring one ethnic or cultural group over another, it can exacerbate tensions and hinder collaborative governance.

Addressing Ethnicity and Culture in Power Dynamics:

Inclusive Governance: Promoting inclusive governance that reflects the diversity of ethnic and cultural groups fosters a sense of representation and reduces feelings of marginalization. Inclusive policies can help mitigate internal conflicts.

Power-Sharing Arrangements: In cases where there are deep-seated ethnic or cultural divisions, power-sharing arrangements may be considered. This involves distributing key political positions among different groups to ensure a more equitable representation.

Cultural Sensitivity in Policy-making: Leaders should be sensitive to the cultural nuances and aspirations of various groups when formulating policies. Recognizing and respecting cultural diversity contributes to more effective and inclusive governance.

Conflict Resolution Mechanisms: Establishing robust conflict resolution mechanisms, including dialogue and mediation processes, can help address internal conflicts arising from ethnic or cultural tensions. Open communication is essential for understanding and resolving grievances.

National Identity Promotion: Fostering a strong sense of national identity that transcends ethnic and cultural differences is vital. This can be achieved through educational programs, shared national symbols, and initiatives that emphasize unity in diversity.

In conclusion, the entwined challenges of corruption, internal conflicts, leadership struggles, and the influence of ethnicity and culture on power dynamics require a holistic and nuanced approach. Reformation efforts should not only address legal and institutional shortcomings but also promote cultural sensitivity, inclusive governance, and conflict resolution mechanisms to foster sustainable stability and development.

Exploration of policies aimed at modernizing key sectors, including finance, industry, and agriculture.

Modernizing key sectors such as finance, industry, and agriculture involves the implementation of strategic policies aimed at enhancing efficiency, productivity, and sustainability. These policies often require a comprehensive approach, considering technological advancements, regulatory frameworks, and capacity-building initiatives. Here's an exploration of policies that can contribute to the modernization of these vital sectors:

Finance Sector Modernization:

Digital Transformation:

- Promote digitalization of financial services to enhance accessibility and efficiency.

- Encourage the use of electronic payment systems, online banking, and mobile financial services.

Regulatory Reforms:

- Establish and update regulations to accommodate fintech innovations.
- Strengthen regulatory frameworks to ensure financial stability and consumer protection.

Financial Inclusion:

- Implement policies to promote financial inclusion, ensuring that a broader population has access to banking and financial services.
- Support the establishment of community banks and mobile banking services in underserved areas.

Capacity Building:

- Invest in training programs for financial professionals to keep pace with technological advancements.
- Foster collaborations between financial institutions and educational institutions to bridge the skills gap.

Industrial Sector Modernization:

Technology Adoption:

- Incentivize industries to adopt advanced technologies such as automation, artificial intelligence, and the Internet of Things (IoT).

- Provide subsidies or tax incentives for businesses investing in modern technologies.

Research and Development (R&D):

- Establish research and development funds to encourage innovation within industries.

- Facilitate collaboration between industries and research institutions to promote technological advancements.

Infrastructure Development:

- Invest in infrastructure projects that support industrial growth, including reliable energy sources, transportation networks, and communication systems.

- Provide incentives for industries adopting green and sustainable practices.

Trade Policies:

- Develop trade policies that foster international collaboration and market access for local industries.

- Encourage the export of high-value-added products to diversify the industrial base.

Agriculture Sector Modernization:

Technology in Agriculture:

- Promote the use of precision farming techniques, IoT devices, and drone technology.

- Facilitate access to agricultural technologies and machinery for smallholder farmers.

Diversification and Value Addition:

- Encourage diversification of crops and livestock to enhance resilience to market fluctuations.

- Support policies that promote value addition, processing, and marketing of agricultural products.

Financial Support:

- Establish agricultural financing programs and credit facilities to support farmers in adopting modern technologies.

- Provide insurance schemes to protect farmers against risks such as climate events and market fluctuations.

Education and Extension Services:

- Invest in agricultural education and extension services to enhance the skills and knowledge of farmers.

- Implement programs that promote sustainable and climate-smart agricultural practices.

Land Reforms:

- Implement land reforms that facilitate efficient land use, reduce fragmentation, and support large-scale modern farming practices.

These policy measures should be adapted to the specific context and challenges of each country or region. Successful modernization requires a collaborative effort involving government agencies, private sectors, and local communities to ensure sustainable and inclusive development across finance, industry, and agriculture sectors.

Examination of the Role of Economic Diversification in Reducing Dependency on Specific Industries:

1. Mitigating Economic Vulnerability:

- Economic diversification helps reduce vulnerability to external shocks. Over-reliance on a single industry exposes a nation to the risks associated with fluctuations in global commodity prices, market demands, or geopolitical events.

2. Enhanced Resilience to Economic Cycles:

- Diversification spreads risk and helps mitigate the impact of economic downturns. When one sector faces challenges, a diversified economy is better equipped to absorb shocks and maintain overall economic stability.

3. Job Creation and Employment Opportunities:

- Diversified economies often generate more employment opportunities across various sectors. This is crucial for social stability and inclusive growth, as it reduces dependence on a specific industry for jobs.

4. Sustainable Development:

- Economic diversification promotes sustainable development by encouraging the growth of industries that align with environmental and social sustainability goals. This can include renewable energy, eco-tourism, and other environmentally friendly sectors.

5. Technology and Innovation Spillovers:

- Diversification encourages the cross-fertilization of ideas and technologies across industries. Innovation in one sector can spill over into others, fostering a culture of creativity and technological advancement.

6. Economic Stability and Fiscal Policy:

- Diversification provides governments with a more stable revenue base. Relying on a single industry for revenues can lead to fiscal volatility, while a diversified economy allows for a more balanced and resilient revenue structure.

7. Global Competitiveness:

- Diversified economies are often more competitive on the global stage. A broad range of industries allows a nation to capitalize on various comparative advantages, making it more adaptable to changes in global markets.

8. Attracting Foreign Direct Investment (FDI):

- Diversified economies tend to attract a broader range of foreign investors. Investors are often attracted to countries with diverse economic opportunities, reducing reliance on specific sectors.

9. Infrastructure Development:

- Economic diversification often necessitates investments in infrastructure development. This, in turn, creates an enabling environment for various industries, contributing to overall economic growth.

10. Improved Standard of Living:

- A diversified economy is more likely to offer a variety of goods and services, contributing to an improved standard of living. A mix of industries can cater to diverse consumer needs and preferences.

Challenges and Considerations:

- **Transition Challenges:** Transitioning from a concentrated to a diversified economy may face resistance and challenges, particularly from vested interests in dominant industries.

- **Resource Reallocation:** Diversification often requires the reallocation of resources, including human capital and financial investments, which can be a complex process.

- **Policy Coordination:** Effective economic diversification requires well-coordinated policies across various sectors. Governments must ensure coherence in their strategies to avoid potential conflicts and unintended consequences.

- **Investment in Education and Training:** Diversifying into new industries may require a skilled workforce. Investment in education and training programs is crucial to ensure the availability of the necessary human capital.

In conclusion, economic diversification plays a pivotal role in reducing dependency on specific industries. It fosters a more resilient, adaptable, and sustainable economy, which is essential for long-term economic growth and stability. Policymakers need to implement measures that encourage diversification while addressing associated challenges to reap the benefits of a more varied and dynamic economic landscape.

Chapter 3: Infrastructure Revolution

Introduction

In-depth look at major infrastructure projects initiated under Biya's administration, including roads, bridges, energy, and telecommunications.

President Paul Biya's administration embarked on a transformative journey marked by a strategic focus on infrastructure development, encompassing roads, bridges, energy, and telecommunications. This chapter offers an in-depth exploration of the major initiatives undertaken, revealing a step-by-step evolution that reshaped Cameroon's physical and technological landscape.

Roads:

The groundwork for this infrastructural metamorphosis began with an ambitious road network expansion. Biya recognized the pivotal role that well-connected roadways play in fostering economic growth and national unity. Projects were meticulously planned, with a focus on enhancing connectivity between urban centers and rural areas. Construction unfolded step by step, linking regions previously isolated and stimulating trade and commerce.

Bridges:

Simultaneously, the administration set its sights on overcoming geographical barriers through the construction of strategic bridges. Each bridge represented a triumph over natural obstacles, facilitating efficient transportation and connectivity. From the design phase to the completion of projects, the development of bridges showcased a commitment to unifying diverse regions and creating a more accessible and integrated nation.

Energy:

Addressing the nation's energy needs, President Biya championed projects that sought to revolutionize the energy sector. Investments in hydroelectric power stations and renewable energy sources marked significant milestones. This step-by-step approach not only expanded energy capacity but also positioned Cameroon as a regional leader in sustainable energy practices, contributing to environmental conservation and reducing dependency on traditional power sources.

Environmental Sustainability and Inclusive Progress: Bridging Gaps in Cameroon's Development

As President Paul Biya's administration meticulously advanced Cameroon's energy capacity, a vital piece of the puzzle emerged — a commitment to sustainable practices and an inclusive vision for progress. The step-by-step approach taken not only expanded energy capabilities but also strategically positioned Cameroon as a regional exemplar in sustainable energy practices. This transformation not only addressed the imperative for environmental conservation but also aimed to bridge historical gaps, ensuring that all tribes and ethnicities were included in the loop of progress.

Sustainable Energy Practices:

At the heart of this approach was the integration of sustainable energy practices. Biya's administration championed the development of hydroelectric power stations and investments in renewable energy sources, leveraging Cameroon's diverse topography for energy production. This step-by-step shift towards sustainability was not merely a technological upgrade but a profound commitment to mitigating environmental impact and safeguarding the nation's natural resources for future generations.

Regional Leadership in Sustainable Energy:

Cameroon's embrace of sustainable energy practices under Biya's leadership positioned the nation as a regional trailblazer. The step-by-step expansion of renewable energy projects not only met domestic needs but also showcased Cameroon's commitment to responsible development on the continental stage. This regional leadership played a dual role — elevating Cameroon's global standing and encouraging neighboring nations to adopt similar eco-friendly practices.

Inclusive Development and Ethnically Diverse Engagement:

Crucially, the chapter unveils a conscientious effort to include all tribes and ethnicities in the progress spurred by sustainable energy projects. Historically marginalized communities found themselves included in the economic benefits of these initiatives. The step-by-step approach was not blind to the unique challenges faced by different ethnic groups, and policies were devised to ensure that the dividends of development reached every corner of the nation.

Empowering Tribal Communities:

Biya's administration introduced targeted programs to empower tribal communities in areas hosting major energy projects. Educational initiatives, vocational training, and employment opportunities were systematically integrated into the development agenda, ensuring that the benefits of progress were not concentrated solely in urban centers but reached the heart of diverse tribal landscapes.

Cultural Preservation alongside Progress:

Recognizing the intrinsic value of Cameroon's cultural diversity, steps were taken to preserve and celebrate the unique traditions of various tribes. Museums, cultural centers, and heritage sites were integrated into the development plans, ensuring that progress did not come at the cost of cultural identity. This step-by-step cultural preservation became a vital aspect of the inclusive vision for Cameroon's future.

This chapter illuminates a holistic approach to progress — one that extends beyond the technical aspects of energy expansion to embrace sustainable practices and inclusive development. By systematically incorporating tribes and ethnicities into the narrative of progress, President Biya's administration sought to redefine development not only in economic terms but as a shared journey towards a more equitable and culturally rich Cameroon.

Telecommunications:

Recognizing the indispensable role of technology in the modern era, Biya's administration prioritized the expansion of the telecommunications infrastructure. Step by step, Cameroon witnessed a digital revolution, with the laying of fiber-optic cables and the establishment of advanced communication networks. This not only connected the nation internally but also positioned Cameroon as a hub for technological advancement within the African continent.

Integrated Development Approach:

What distinguished Biya's approach was the interconnectedness of these projects. Roads facilitated the transportation of materials and personnel for energy and telecommunication endeavors. Bridges enhanced accessibility to energy projects in remote areas. This integrated development strategy showcased a holistic understanding of the symbiotic relationship between different facets of infrastructure.

This chapter, therefore, unveils a meticulously executed plan that unfolded step by step, portraying President Biya's commitment to catapulting Cameroon into a new era of connectivity and technological advancement. Through roads, bridges, energy, and telecommunications, Biya's administration laid the foundation for a more interconnected, resilient, and forward-looking nation.

As President Paul Biya's administration ushered in progress through sustainable energy projects, a crucial aspect emerged — the preservation of tribal laws and values. The step-by-step approach taken not only prioritized economic benefits but also ensured that the cultural fabric of diverse tribal landscapes remained intact. This commitment aimed to dispel the historical trend of concentrating progress solely in urban centers, affirming that the benefits of development reached the very heart of Cameroon's varied tribal communities.

Integration of Tribal Laws into Development Policies:

The chapter delves into the deliberate efforts made by Biya's administration to integrate tribal laws into the broader framework of development policies. Rather than imposing a one-size-fits-all approach, the step-by-step strategy acknowledged the unique legal and customary systems of different tribes. This inclusive approach allowed for a more nuanced and sustainable model of progress that respected the distinctiveness of each tribal landscape.

Community-Based Decision-Making Structures:

Recognizing the importance of community engagement, the administration established community-based decision-making structures. These structures, integrated into the development process, allowed tribes to actively participate in shaping the trajectory of progress. By incorporating local perspectives and adhering to tribal laws, the step-by-step integration fostered a sense of ownership and empowerment among diverse communities.

Empowering Tribal Leaders as Guardians of Tradition:

The chapter unfolds a strategic initiative to empower tribal leaders as guardians of tradition. Biya's administration recognized these leaders as invaluable stewards of cultural heritage and sought to amplify their role in the development discourse. By involving them in decision-making processes, the step-by-step progression not only preserved tribal values but elevated traditional leaders as vital contributors to the nation's progress.

Cultural Education Initiatives:

Parallel to economic advancements, the chapter explores educational initiatives designed to preserve and promote tribal cultures. Museums, cultural centers, and educational programs were systematically introduced, providing platforms for the transmission of tribal values to younger generations. The step-by-step cultural education became an integral part of sustainable progress, ensuring that the rich tapestry of Cameroon's cultural diversity remained vibrant.

Economic Opportunities in Tribal Landscapes:

The inclusive vision extended beyond mere cultural preservation to economic empowerment. Economic opportunities were strategically introduced in tribal landscapes, with a focus on sustainable practices that aligned with tribal values. The step-by-step economic integration aimed to uplift tribes economically without compromising their cultural identity.

By meticulously incorporating the subtleties of tribal laws and values into the development narrative, this chapter reveals how President Biya's administration sought not only to bring progress to diverse tribal landscapes but also to ensure that this progress was deeply rooted, sustainable, and respectful of the invaluable cultural heritage woven into the very fabric of Cameroon's tribal communities.

Evaluation of the impact of these projects on regional connectivity, trade, and overall economic development.

Infrastructure Revolution: Impact on Regional Connectivity, Trade, and Economic Development

President Paul Biya's ambitious infrastructure projects, spanning roads, bridges, energy, and telecommunications, were not just about physical construction but aimed at reshaping the political, economic, and social landscape of Cameroon. This chapter evaluates the multifaceted impact of these projects on regional connectivity, trade, and overall economic development, taking into account both the domestic political environment and international perspectives.

Regional Connectivity:

The step-by-step development of roads and bridges significantly enhanced regional connectivity. Remote areas were integrated into the national fabric, fostering a sense of unity and cohesiveness. The chapter explores how improved transportation infrastructure facilitated the movement of people and goods, reducing travel times and enhancing accessibility to previously isolated regions. The resulting interconnectedness not only strengthened internal ties but also positioned Cameroon as a more cohesive regional entity.

Trade Facilitation:

An integral outcome of enhanced regional connectivity was the facilitation of trade. This chapter delves into the ways in which upgraded roads and bridges streamlined the movement of goods, fostering economic activity. The step-by-step progress in infrastructure development is examined in relation to the expansion of trade networks, both domestically and internationally. Through case studies and economic indicators, the chapter evaluates the impact on trade balance and the overall vibrancy of Cameroon's economy.

Overall Economic Development:

The transformative effect of these infrastructure projects on Cameroon's economic development is a central focus. The chapter analyzes how the improved energy infrastructure and telecommunications networks stimulated economic growth, attracting investments and fostering innovation. By examining key economic indicators, employment rates, and GDP growth, the impact of these developments on the nation's overall economic health is evaluated.

Political Environment:

The political implications of these infrastructure projects are explored within the context of Cameroon's internal politics. The chapter examines how the projects influenced public opinion, the government's popularity, and political stability. By considering how these developments aligned with or challenged existing political narratives, it evaluates their role in shaping the domestic political environment.

International Perspectives:

Beyond domestic considerations, this chapter scrutinizes how these infrastructure initiatives were perceived by other nations. By examining diplomatic relations, international partnerships formed, and the global image of Cameroon, the chapter sheds light on how these projects influenced the nation's standing on the world stage. It considers whether Cameroon's step-by-step progress garnered admiration or criticism and how these international perceptions impacted foreign relations.

In summary, this chapter provides a comprehensive evaluation of the transformative impact of infrastructure projects on regional connectivity, trade, and overall economic development. By examining the interplay of domestic and international factors, it presents a nuanced understanding of how these initiatives not only reshaped Cameroon's physical landscape but also influenced its political and economic trajectory.

Conclusion

Conclusively examining the landscape of creative thinking and communication in Cameroon, Africa, particularly in the context of perceived issues related to the lack of responsibility and accountability, involves acknowledging both the positive strides and the challenges that characterize this dynamic environment.

Creative Thinking:

Cultural Richness:

- Cameroon, with its diverse cultures and languages, offers a rich tapestry for creative expression. The amalgamation of traditional and modern influences creates a unique foundation for innovative thinking.

Youth Entrepreneurship:

- The youth in Cameroon demonstrate creative potential, particularly in the entrepreneurial sphere. Initiatives aimed at harnessing this creativity have shown promise in fostering economic growth and sustainability.

Artistic Expression:

- Cameroon boasts a vibrant arts scene, encompassing music, literature, and visual arts. Artists often use their work to address social issues and challenge societal norms.

Digital Innovation:

- The country has witnessed a rise in digital innovation, with tech startups emerging and contributing to the digital economy. This reflects an evolving mindset towards embracing technological advancements.

Communication:

Media Landscape:

- The media landscape in Cameroon plays a crucial role in communication. However, concerns about press freedom and restrictions on journalistic activities have been raised, impacting the free flow of information.

Social Media Influence:

- Social media platforms have become significant channels for communication, allowing citizens to express opinions and share information. However, there have been instances of government restrictions on internet access during times of political unrest.

Government Communication:

- The government's communication strategies, at times, have been criticized for lack of transparency and accountability. Access to information, especially related to governance and public spending, remains a challenge.

Civil Society Engagement:

- Civil society organizations and advocacy groups play a vital role in communication efforts. They often act as conduits for citizen voices and contribute to shaping public discourse.

Lack of Responsibility and Accountability:

Corruption Concerns:

- Instances of corruption within public institutions have been reported, impacting the effective implementation of policies and hindering development efforts.

Governance Challenges:

- The country has faced governance challenges, with some segments of the population feeling marginalized. This has led to calls for more inclusive governance structures.

Limited Transparency:

- There are concerns about the lack of transparency in government actions and decisions. Access to information, especially concerning public resources, can be limited.

Judicial Independence:

- The independence of the judiciary has been questioned, affecting its ability to act as a check on the executive branch and ensure accountability.

Conclusion:

In conclusion, while Cameroon showcases remarkable creativity and potential for innovation, challenges persist in the realms of communication, responsibility, and accountability. Addressing these challenges requires concerted efforts from both the government and civil society to foster an environment that encourages open dialogue, transparency, and a commitment to responsible governance. The trajectory of creative thinking and communication in Cameroon holds promise, and positive change is contingent upon embracing inclusivity, transparency, and accountability as integral components of the national narrative.

Chapter 4: Social Development Programs

Overview of social welfare programs implemented to improve healthcare, education, and poverty alleviation.

It appears you're asking for an overview of hypothetical social welfare programs for healthcare, education, and poverty alleviation, as well as the development of a new ethnicity. While the concept of creating an entirely new ethnicity is not feasible in reality, for the purpose of your inquiry, I'll provide a creative and hypothetical scenario.

Social Welfare Programs:

1. Healthcare Improvement Program - "HealthyCommunities"

Problem Solving:

- **Objective:** To enhance healthcare accessibility and quality for all residents.

- **Components:**

    - Establish community health centers in underserved areas.

    - Provide financial incentives for healthcare professionals working in these centers.

    - Implement preventive health education campaigns.

2. Education Enhancement Initiative - "FutureBuilders"

- **Objective:** To improve educational opportunities and outcomes for all, with a focus on marginalized communities.

- **Components:**

    - Introduce after-school programs for additional learning support.

    - Provide scholarships and financial aid for students in low-income households.

- Implement mentorship programs to guide students through their academic journey.

3. Poverty Alleviation Strategy - "OpportunityRise"

- **Objective:** To break the cycle of poverty and empower individuals and families.

- **Components:**

    - Establish vocational training centers for skill development.

    - Create a microfinance program to support small businesses.

    - Develop a comprehensive job placement and career counseling service.

New Ethnicity Development:

1. Cultural Identity Program - "UnityCultures"

- **Objective:** To celebrate diversity and foster a sense of unity among diverse populations.

- **Components:**

    - Promote cultural exchange events to share traditions and histories.

    - Establish cultural awareness programs in schools and workplaces.

- Develop a national holiday celebrating cultural diversity.

2. Ethnicity-Inclusive Policies - "EqualHeritage"

- **Objective:** To ensure equal opportunities and representation for all ethnic groups.

- **Components:**

  - Implement affirmative action policies in education and employment.

  - Establish cultural sensitivity training for public service providers.

  - Develop a national database to monitor and address ethnic disparities.

3. Social Harmony Initiative - "HarmonyNation"

- **Objective:** To build a cohesive society where individuals of all backgrounds coexist peacefully.

- **Components:**

  - Implement community-building projects that involve all ethnic groups.

  - Facilitate intercultural dialogue forums and events.

  - Develop a curriculum in schools promoting understanding and respect for different ethnicities.

Evaluation and Monitoring:

- Regularly assess the impact of social welfare programs through data collection and analysis.

- Encourage community feedback to identify areas for improvement and additional support.

- Establish an independent oversight committee to ensure transparency and accountability in program implementation.

While these programs are hypothetical, they reflect common elements found in successful real-world initiatives. In practice, implementing and sustaining such programs would require collaboration between government agencies, non-profit organizations, and community stakeholders. Additionally, the development of a new ethnicity is a complex and sensitive matter that goes beyond the scope of practical implementation. It's crucial to prioritize inclusive policies and practices that celebrate existing diversity and promote unity.

It is important to approach the concept of "EqualHeritage" or any ethnicity-inclusive policies with sensitivity and a commitment to human rights and ethical principles. While promoting inclusivity and equality is admirable, manipulating traditional practices or religious beliefs raises ethical concerns and may infringe upon individual rights. Policies should be designed to foster understanding, respect, and harmony among diverse ethnic and religious groups rather than manipulating them. Here's a perspective that emphasizes inclusivity without manipulation:

Ethnicity-Inclusive Policies - "EqualHeritage": TRADITIONAL LAW

Cultural Appreciation:

- **Objective:** Foster mutual understanding and appreciation for diverse cultures and traditions.

- **Approach:** Encourage cultural exchange programs, heritage festivals, and educational initiatives that highlight the richness of each ethnic group's heritage.

Religious Tolerance:

- **Objective:** Promote tolerance and respect for different religious beliefs.

- **Approach:** Facilitate interfaith dialogue forums, educational programs on religious diversity, and initiatives that emphasize shared values.

Affirmative Action for Equality:

- **Objective:** Address historical disparities and promote equal opportunities.

- **Approach:** Implement affirmative action policies that ensure fair representation and access to resources for historically marginalized ethnic groups without manipulating traditions or religions.

Inclusive Educational Curriculum:

- **Objective:** Provide an education that reflects the diversity of the nation's history and cultures.

- **Approach:** Develop curricula that include contributions from various ethnic and religious groups, promoting a sense of belonging and shared national identity.

Community-Led Development:

- **Objective:** Empower communities to actively participate in their development.

- **Approach:** Facilitate community-led initiatives, involving diverse ethnic and religious leaders in decision-making processes for sustainable development.

Legal Protections Against Discrimination:

- **Objective:** Ensure legal protections against ethnic and religious discrimination.

- **Approach:** Enforce and strengthen anti-discrimination laws, promoting a legal framework that upholds the rights of all citizens, regardless of their ethnic or religious background.

Promotion of Unity:

- **Objective:** Cultivate a sense of national unity.

- **Approach:** Develop campaigns that celebrate national unity, focusing on common values and shared aspirations, rather than manipulating traditional or religious practices.

Conflict Resolution Mechanisms:

- **Objective:** Address conflicts arising from ethnic or religious differences.

- **Approach:** Establish effective conflict resolution mechanisms that emphasize dialogue, mediation, and reconciliation to build understanding among different communities.

Access to Healthcare and Social Services:

- **Objective:** Ensure equitable access to healthcare and social services for all citizens.

- **Approach:** Implement policies that address healthcare disparities in marginalized communities, focusing on health education and service delivery.

Preservation of Cultural Heritage:

- **Objective:** Preserve and celebrate cultural heritage without manipulation.

- **Approach:** Support initiatives for the preservation of cultural heritage, such as museums, cultural centers, and festivals that respect the authenticity of traditions.

In summary, promoting equality and inclusivity should be approached with the utmost respect for individual rights and the autonomy of cultural and religious practices. Policies should aim to unite communities rather than manipulate traditions or beliefs, fostering a society where diversity is celebrated and every citizen can contribute to the nation's progress.

Workshop and Case studies and success stories highlighting the impact of these programs on the lives of the Cameroonian people.

WORKSHOP

Creating workshops, case studies, and success stories to highlight the impact of programs on the lives of the Cameroonian people involves a comprehensive approach that considers the unique context of Cameroon, including its political landscape shaped by President Paul Biya's leadership and the philosophical underpinnings often associated with "Biyaism."

Here's a step-by-step guide:

Step 1: Define Workshop Objectives

Objective Setting:

- Clearly define the objectives of the workshop, such as promoting understanding of the implemented programs, sharing success stories, and fostering dialogue on Biyaism philosophy.

Target Audience:

- Identify the target audience, including government officials, community leaders, NGOs, and the general public.

Step 2: Program Overview

Program Overview Session:

- Conduct a session providing a comprehensive overview of the implemented programs in healthcare, education, and poverty alleviation.

Case Study Selection:

- Choose specific cases that represent successful outcomes in each program area. Highlight diverse examples to show the broad impact.

Step 3: Success Stories

Interactive Storytelling:

- Use interactive storytelling methods to share success stories. Incorporate testimonials from individuals whose lives have been positively impacted.

Media Integration:

- Integrate multimedia elements such as videos, photos, and interviews to visually illustrate success stories.

Step 4: Biyaism Philosophy

Philosophy Introduction:

- Provide an introduction to Biyaism philosophy, emphasizing its key principles, including political stability, economic development, and social harmony.

Expert Insights:

- Invite experts or scholars to offer insights into the interpretation of Biyaism, considering its historical context and evolution over time.

Step 5: Panel Discussions

Panel Discussions:

- Organize panel discussions involving policymakers, program implementers, and beneficiaries to provide diverse perspectives on the impact of programs and the role of Biyaism.

Q&A Session:

- Facilitate a question-and-answer session allowing participants to engage directly with the panelists, fostering a deeper understanding.

Step 6: Workshop Activities

Group Activities:

- Organize group activities to encourage participants to brainstorm ideas for further program improvement or expansion.

Interactive Workshops:

- Conduct interactive workshops focused on key themes, such as community engagement, sustainable development, and inclusive governance.

Step 7: Evaluation and Feedback

Feedback Sessions:

- Collect feedback from participants to gauge the effectiveness of
  the workshop and identify areas for improvement.

Evaluation of Impact:

- Evaluate the impact of the workshop by tracking subsequent
  actions or initiatives inspired by the discussions.

Step 8: Documentation and Dissemination

Documentation:

- Document the workshop proceedings, including key
  discussions, success stories, and recommendations.

Dissemination:

- Disseminate the workshop outcomes through various channels,
  such as reports, articles, and social media platforms.

Step 9: Follow-Up Initiatives

Follow-Up Initiatives:

- Implement follow-up initiatives, such as regular forums or
  newsletters, to sustain the momentum and continue the
  dialogue.

Adaptation of Programs:

- Use feedback from the workshop to adapt and enhance existing programs based on the needs and suggestions of the community.

By following these steps, the workshop can serve as a platform for constructive dialogue, knowledge sharing, and the celebration of positive outcomes. Emphasizing the impact of programs on the lives of the Cameroonian people while incorporating insights into Biyaism philosophy can contribute to a more comprehensive understanding of governance and development in Cameroon.

Chapter 5: Foreign Relations and Economic Diplomacy

Introduction

- Exploration of Biya's strategies for attracting foreign investment and fostering economic partnerships.

As of my last knowledge update in January 2012, Paul Biya was the President of Cameroon, having been in office since 1982. Strategies for attracting foreign investment and fostering economic partnerships are crucial aspects of any government's economic policy. However, it's important to note that the specific strategies employed by President Biya may have evolved continually from the change of the public ministers of affair and Director or changed since then. Here is an exploration of general strategies that leaders, including Paul Biya, may use to attract foreign investment and build economic partnerships: Not very strong because of the multiple change and consistency changing the boundaries of the contract and economic behavior.

Attracting Foreign Investment:

Political Stability:

- Stability in governance is crucial for attracting foreign investment. President Biya may focus on maintaining political stability and implementing policies that create a favorable business environment.

Economic Reforms:

- Implementing economic reforms to liberalize markets, simplify regulations, and improve the ease of doing business can attract foreign investors.

Infrastructure Development:

- Investing in critical infrastructure, such as transportation, energy, and telecommunications, can make the country more attractive to foreign investors.

Incentive Programs:

- Offering financial incentives, tax breaks, or other perks to foreign investors can encourage them to invest in the country.

Sector-Specific Promotion:

- Identifying key sectors for development and actively promoting investment in those areas, such as agriculture, technology, or energy, can attract targeted foreign investment.

Fostering Economic Partnerships:

Diplomatic Engagements:

- Engaging in diplomatic efforts to build relationships with other countries is essential. This involves participating in international forums and establishing bilateral agreements.

Trade Agreements:

- Negotiating and signing trade agreements can open up markets, increase exports, and foster economic partnerships with other nations.

Investment Promotion Agencies:

- Establishing or strengthening investment promotion agencies can actively seek out potential investors and promote the country as an attractive investment destination.

Global Economic Forums:

- Participating in global economic forums provides opportunities to showcase the country's economic potential and engage with international business leaders.

Partnership Initiatives:

- Initiating and participating in international partnerships, such as development projects or joint ventures, can enhance economic cooperation.

Historical Context - Francois Mitterrand and Ronald Reagan Diplomacy:

Francois Mitterrand (France):

- **European Integration:** Mitterrand was a strong advocate for European integration and worked towards strengthening the European Union.

- **Socialist Economic Policies:** While pursuing socialist economic policies domestically, Mitterrand also recognized the importance of a competitive and open global economy with his colonies not partnerships.

- **International Relations:** Mitterrand was actively engaged in international diplomacy, and reducing the power of the CFA including efforts to foster cooperation within the European community and managing relations with the United States during the Cold War. and Making Africa, particularly Cameroon, the source of natural productivity.

Ronald Reagan (United States):

- **Economic Policies:** Reagan implemented supply-side economic policies, known as "Reaganomics," which aimed to stimulate economic growth through tax cuts and deregulation.

- **Anti-Communism Stance:** Reagan took a strong anti-communist stance during the Cold War and implemented policies to counter Soviet influence globally. Presenting the IMAGE OF CHINA as the monster of the ECONOMY.

- **Diplomacy and Arms Reduction:** Reagan engaged in diplomatic efforts with the Soviet Union, leading to arms reduction agreements, such as the Intermediate-Range Nuclear Forces (INF) Treaty. This does affect Cameroon to end over his ability to build in own army and develop his own national security

Coup D'Etat:

- A coup d'etat refers to the sudden overthrow of a government, often involving military forces.

- It's crucial to note that the legitimacy and ethical implications of a coup can vary widely based on the circumstances and the intentions of those involved.

- Coup d'etats can have significant political, social, and economic consequences, impacting stability and deterring foreign investment.

- POLITICAL IMPACT IN FAVOR:

- SOCIAL IMPACT

- ECONOMICAL CONSEQUENCES

In summary, attracting foreign investment and fostering economic partnerships typically involve a combination of political stability, economic reforms, infrastructure development, and diplomatic efforts. Each leader's approach is influenced by their unique geopolitical context, economic philosophy, and national priorities. It's essential to consider the evolving nature of political dynamics and global economic conditions when analyzing the strategies employed by leaders like Paul Biya, Francois Mitterrand, and Ronald Reagan.

Analysis of trade policies and international collaborations that contributed to Cameroon's economic growth.

However, I can provide a general analysis of trade policies and international collaborations that may have contributed to Cameroon's economic growth. Keep in mind that this analysis is based on general economic principles and historical trends up to 2022:

Trade Policies and International Collaborations:

Diversification of Trade Partners:

- Cameroon has sought to diversify its trade partners to reduce dependency on a single market. Engaging with a diverse set of countries can help mitigate economic risks and enhance market access.

Regional Economic Integration:

- Membership in regional economic communities, such as the Economic Community of Central African States (ECCAS) and the Central African Economic and Monetary Community (CEMAC), facilitates intra-regional trade and economic cooperation.

Trade Agreements:

- Negotiating and signing trade agreements with various countries and regional blocs can create preferential trade conditions, opening up new markets and promoting exports.

Investment Promotion:

- Implementing policies that attract foreign direct investment (FDI) can contribute to economic growth. Cameroon has taken steps to improve its business environment, offering incentives to foreign investors.

Infrastructure Development:

- Upgrading transportation and logistics infrastructure, such as ports and roads, enhances the efficiency of trade activities. Improved infrastructure supports export capabilities and attracts investment.

Export Diversification:

- Encouraging and supporting the diversification of exports beyond traditional commodities can increase resilience to market fluctuations and contribute to sustained economic growth.

Collaboration with Development Partners:

- Collaborating with international organizations and development partners on projects related to infrastructure, education, and healthcare can contribute to overall economic development.

Compliance with International Standards:

- Aligning with international standards and regulations enhances Cameroon's competitiveness in global markets. It demonstrates a commitment to quality and reliability.

Technology Transfer and Innovation:

- Collaborating with technologically advanced nations allows for the transfer of technology and knowledge, fostering innovation and increasing productivity.

Analysis of Other Resistances or Coups:

Regarding any potential resistance or coup within the Cameroon army after 1982, it's crucial to note that political and military dynamics can be sensitive topics. Cameroon has experienced periods of political stability under President Paul Biya's long tenure, but there have also been challenges, particularly in regions like the Anglophone areas.

Anglophone Crisis:

- One notable challenge has been the Anglophone Crisis, marked by tensions and violence in English-speaking regions. This unrest is rooted in historical, linguistic, and political grievances and has posed challenges to the government's authority.

Security Concerns:

- The Boko Haram insurgency in the northern regions and security concerns along the border with Nigeria have been significant challenges, necessitating military responses.

Political Opposition:

- While Cameroon has experienced some political opposition, President Biya has maintained a firm grip on power. Allegations of electoral irregularities and opposition claims of political repression have been raised.

Military Loyalty:

- The loyalty of the military has been crucial in maintaining political stability. Any potential resistance or coup within the army would depend on various factors, including internal dynamics and political allegiances.

It's important to approach discussions on political and military events with a nuanced understanding of the context, considering various perspectives and relying on accurate and up-to-date sources for the latest information. Political situations can evolve, and events may have transpired since my last update in January 2022.

- Examination of challenges faced in navigating the global economic landscape.

As of my last knowledge update in January 2012, by 2020 his administration has improved in creating new systems to improve the ability to deal with law and collaborate with business management. I don't have specific information on recent military reforms undertaken by President Paul Biya in Cameroon. Military reforms can encompass a range of initiatives, including organizational restructuring, modernization efforts, and training programs. To provide a comprehensive analysis, let's examine potential challenges faced by Cameroon in navigating the global economic landscape:

Challenges in Navigating the Global Economic Landscape:

Economic Diversification:

- **Challenge:** Cameroon's economy is heavily reliant on oil and agricultural commodities. Diversifying the economy to reduce dependence on a few sectors poses a challenge, especially in the face of fluctuating commodity prices in the global market.

Trade Imbalances:

- **Challenge:** Maintaining a favorable balance of trade can be challenging, particularly if the country faces trade deficits.

Addressing imbalances requires strategic trade policies and efforts to enhance export capabilities.

Infrastructure Deficiencies:

- **Challenge:** Inadequate infrastructure, including transportation and energy systems, can hinder economic development and competitiveness. Addressing infrastructure deficiencies requires substantial investments and effective project implementation. The structure of any part of the development cities and constructive enhancement.

Access to Finance:

- **Challenge:** Small and medium-sized enterprises (SMEs) may face challenges in accessing affordable financing. Improving financial inclusivity and facilitating access to credit are crucial for fostering entrepreneurship and economic growth.

Global Market Volatility:

- **Challenge:** Global economic uncertainties and market volatilities can impact Cameroon's export earnings and foreign exchange reserves. Developing strategies to mitigate the impact of external shocks is essential.

Political Stability and Governance:

- **Challenge:** Ensuring political stability and effective governance is critical for attracting foreign investment and fostering economic growth. Political unrest or governance issues can deter investors and disrupt economic activities.

Climate Change Impact:

- **Challenge:** Cameroon, like many African nations, is vulnerable to the impacts of climate change, affecting agriculture and natural resources. Developing adaptive strategies and sustainable practices is crucial for long-term resilience.

Youth Unemployment:

- **Challenge:** High levels of youth unemployment pose a social and economic challenge. Implementing effective job creation programs and vocational training initiatives is necessary to harness the potential of the youth demographic.

Digital Divide:

- **Challenge:** Bridging the digital divide is crucial for participating in the global digital economy. Enhancing digital infrastructure and promoting digital literacy are essential components of a modern economy.

Global Health Crises:

- **Challenge:** Events like the COVID-19 pandemic can disrupt global supply chains and impact economic activities. Developing robust healthcare systems and contingency plans is crucial for mitigating the impact of health crises.

Military Reformation:

While specific details on military reforms under President Biya are not available, hypothetical challenges in military reformation might include:

Budgetary Constraints:

- **Challenge:** Allocating sufficient funds for military modernization amid competing budgetary priorities can be challenging.

Technology Integration:

- **Challenge:** Integrating modern technologies into the military may face hurdles such as infrastructure limitations and the need for specialized training.

Personnel Training and Welfare:

- **Challenge:** Ensuring adequate training and welfare for military personnel is crucial. This includes addressing issues related to recruitment, retention, and morale.

Adaptability to New Threats:

- **Challenge:** The military must be adaptable to evolving security threats, including cyber threats, terrorism, and unconventional warfare. Open source colonialism military openness toward the nation's civil rights.

Civil-Military Relations:

- **Challenge:** Maintaining a balance in civil-military relations is crucial to avoid potential political tensions between England,France and western military corporations.

Coordination with Regional Partners:

- **Challenge:** Ensuring effective coordination with regional partners to address shared security concerns is essential.

Human Rights Considerations:

- **Challenge:** Balancing security needs with human rights considerations is important to avoid international criticism.

Strategic Planning:

- **Challenge:** Developing and implementing a comprehensive strategic plan for the military requires careful analysis and foresight.

It's important to note that specific details on military reforms and economic challenges may have changed since my last update, and the analysis provided is based on general principles and historical trends up to January 2012. For the latest and most accurate information, consulting recent sources is recommended.

Chapter 6: Challenges and Controversies in Economic Management

Introduction:

Candid discussion of economic challenges faced by Biya's administration.

Cameroon, like many nations, faces various economic challenges that impact different cities across the country. The economic challenges are complex and multifaceted, influenced by factors such as global market conditions, internal governance, and regional disparities. While I cannot provide a discussion specific to each city, I can highlight some overarching economic challenges faced by the administration of President Paul Biya in Cameroon:

1. Oil Dependency:

- **Challenge:** The economy has historically been reliant on oil exports. Fluctuations in global oil prices impact revenue, and a heavy dependence on a single commodity poses risks to economic stability.

2. Agricultural Sector Struggles:

- **Challenge:** Despite being a significant contributor to employment, the agricultural sector faces challenges, including inadequate infrastructure, low productivity, and vulnerability to climate change.

The challenges facing the agricultural sector in Cameroon are complex and interconnected, impacting the sector's overall productivity and its ability to contribute to employment and economic development. Let's delve deeper into the specific challenges mentioned:

1. Inadequate Infrastructure:

- **Issue:** Poor infrastructure, particularly in rural areas, hampers the agricultural supply chain. Insufficient road networks, storage facilities, and irrigation systems make it difficult for farmers to transport produce, store it effectively, and ensure consistent water supply for crops.

- **Impact:** Inadequate infrastructure increases post-harvest losses, limits access to markets, and reduces the overall efficiency of agricultural activities. Farmers may face difficulties in reaching consumers or getting their products to urban centers.

2. Low Productivity:

- **Issue:** Low agricultural productivity can be attributed to various factors, including outdated farming practices, limited access to modern technology, inadequate extension services, and challenges in obtaining quality inputs such as seeds and fertilizers.

- **Impact:** Low productivity means that farmers may not maximize their yield potential. This affects their income, food security, and the overall contribution of the agricultural sector to the economy. It also makes farmers more vulnerable to external shocks.

3. Vulnerability to Climate Change:

- **Issue:** Climate change poses a significant threat to agriculture, leading to unpredictable weather patterns, increased frequency of extreme events (droughts, floods), and the spread of pests and diseases. Smallholder farmers, in particular, may lack resources to adapt to these changes.
- **Impact:** Erratic weather patterns can result in crop failures, reduced yields, and increased susceptibility to pests and diseases. This vulnerability undermines the resilience of the agricultural sector and threatens food security.

4. Access to Finance:

- **Issue:** Limited access to financial resources hinders farmers' ability to invest in modern agricultural practices, purchase quality inputs, and adopt new technologies. Financial institutions may be hesitant to lend to smallholder farmers due to perceived risks.
- **Impact:** Lack of access to finance constrains farmers' capacity to modernize their operations, improve productivity, and cope with the

impacts of climate change. It perpetuates a cycle of low investment and limited growth in the sector.

5. Market Access Challenges:

- **Issue:** Farmers often face difficulties accessing markets due to inadequate transportation infrastructure, information gaps, and limited market linkages. Middlemen may exploit this situation, resulting in lower profits for farmers.

- **Impact:** Limited market access can lead to reduced income for farmers and discourage them from investing in their farms. It also contributes to a lack of incentive for adopting modern and efficient farming practices.

6. Land Tenure Issues:

- **Issue:** Uncertain land tenure arrangements can lead to land disputes and inhibit long-term investments in agriculture. Lack of clear property rights may discourage farmers from making sustainable land management decisions.

- **Impact:** Land tenure issues can impede agricultural development and discourage farmers from making long-term investments. This hinders efforts to implement sustainable and efficient farming practices.

Addressing these challenges requires a holistic approach that involves government intervention, private sector collaboration, and support from international partners. Investments in infrastructure, technology transfer, climate-resilient farming practices, and financial inclusion for farmers are crucial components of a strategy to enhance the productivity and sustainability of the agricultural sector in Cameroon.

3. Infrastructure Deficiencies:

- **Challenge:** Insufficient infrastructure, particularly in transportation and energy, hampers economic development. Poor road networks and unreliable power supply can deter investment and hinder business operations.

4. Youth Unemployment:

- **Challenge:** High levels of youth unemployment are a pressing issue. The job market struggles to absorb the growing youth population, leading to social and economic challenges.

5. Regional Disparities:

- **Challenge:** There are notable regional disparities in economic development. The northern regions, for example, face greater challenges in terms of poverty and lack of access to essential services compared to the more prosperous southern regions.

6. Corruption and Governance Issues:

- **Challenge:** Concerns about corruption and governance issues have been raised. Addressing these challenges is crucial for creating a transparent and conducive environment for business and investment.

7. Foreign Debt Burden:

- **Challenge:** The country carries a substantial external debt burden. Servicing this debt can strain public finances, limiting the government's ability to invest in critical sectors.

8. Global Economic Downturns:

- **Challenge:** The global economic landscape, including economic downturns and external shocks, impacts Cameroon's export earnings and overall economic performance.

9. Security Concerns:

- **Challenge:** Security challenges, including the Boko Haram insurgency in the northern regions and the Anglophone Crisis, have economic implications, affecting livelihoods, displacing populations, and disrupting economic activities.

10. Informal Economy Dominance:

- **Challenge:** A significant portion of economic activity occurs in the informal sector. While this sector contributes to employment, it also poses challenges for revenue collection and regulatory oversight.

11. Access to Finance:

- **Challenge:** Limited access to finance for small and medium-sized enterprises (SMEs) constrains entrepreneurship and economic diversification.

The challenge of insufficient infrastructure, especially in transportation and energy, is a significant obstacle to economic development in many countries, including Cameroon. Let's explore the specific issues related to inadequate infrastructure and their impact on economic growth:

1. Poor Road Networks:

- **Issue:** Inadequate and poorly maintained road networks limit the efficient movement of goods and people. This can result in higher transportation costs, longer delivery times, and increased wear and tear on vehicles.
- **Impact:** Businesses face challenges in transporting raw materials and finished goods, leading to increased production costs. Poor road connectivity can also hinder market access for farmers, limiting their ability to sell products beyond local markets.

2. Unreliable Power Supply:

- **Issue:** Insufficient and unreliable energy supply, including electricity, can disrupt industrial operations, affecting manufacturing and productivity. Frequent power outages and fluctuations can damage machinery and equipment.
- **Impact:** Industries may face production delays, increased operational costs due to the need for backup power sources, and reduced overall productivity. This can deter both domestic and foreign investment.

3. Impact on Investment:

- **Challenge:** The lack of robust transportation and energy infrastructure can discourage private sector investment. Investors may be reluctant to commit capital to regions with poor connectivity and unreliable power supply.

- **Impact:** Reduced investment limits economic growth opportunities. Industries that require efficient transportation and energy infrastructure, such as manufacturing and logistics, may be hesitant to establish or expand operations in areas with inadequate facilities.

4. Rural-Urban Disparities:

- **Challenge:** Inadequate infrastructure often leads to disparities between rural and urban areas. Urban centers may have better connectivity and more reliable energy supply, exacerbating regional economic inequalities.

- **Impact:** Rural areas may face challenges in accessing markets, education, and healthcare services. The urban-rural divide can hinder inclusive economic development and contribute to social disparities.

5. Logistics and Supply Chain Challenges:

- **Challenge:** Poor transportation infrastructure affects the efficiency of logistics and supply chains. Delays in transporting goods can result in inventory issues and increased costs.

- **Impact:** Businesses may struggle to maintain optimal inventory levels, affecting their ability to meet customer demands promptly. This can lead to inefficiencies and reduced competitiveness.

6. Inhibitor of Export Competitiveness:

- **Challenge:** Insufficient infrastructure can hinder a country's export competitiveness. Export-oriented industries may face challenges in getting products to ports efficiently.
- **Impact:** Limited export competitiveness can impede economic growth, as countries may struggle to take full advantage of international trade opportunities. This is particularly crucial in a globalized economy.

7. High Transportation Costs:

- **Challenge:** Poor transportation infrastructure can lead to higher transportation costs, affecting the overall cost structure of goods and services.
- **Impact:** Increased transportation costs can reduce the competitiveness of domestically produced goods in both domestic and international markets. It also puts pressure on businesses, leading to lower profit margins.

8. Investor Confidence and Business Operations:

- **Challenge:** Insufficient infrastructure can erode investor confidence and impact the day-to-day operations of businesses. Investors may be concerned about the reliability and cost-effectiveness of operations.
- **Impact:** Businesses may face challenges in attracting and retaining investors. The lack of reliable infrastructure can hinder long-term business planning and expansion efforts.

Addressing these infrastructure challenges requires concerted efforts from the government, private sector, and international partners. Investments in the construction and maintenance of road networks, development of reliable energy sources, and the implementation of policies to improve overall infrastructure are essential for fostering economic development and attracting investment in Cameroon.

12. Healthcare Infrastructure:

- **Challenge:** Inadequate healthcare infrastructure, highlighted during health crises like the COVID-19 pandemic, can impact workforce productivity and strain public resources.

13. Education Quality and Access:

- **Challenge:** Ensuring quality education and access to educational opportunities is crucial for developing a skilled workforce. Challenges in the education sector can hinder human capital development.

14. Land Tenure Issues:

- **Challenge:** Land tenure issues can impact agricultural productivity and hinder investment in certain sectors.

15. Digital Divide:

- **Challenge:** Bridging the digital divide is essential for participating in the global digital economy. Unequal access to digital resources can hinder economic growth.

It's important to note that the impact and severity of these challenges can vary across cities and regions in Cameroon. Addressing these issues requires comprehensive and targeted policies, regional development strategies, and international collaboration. Additionally, developments may have occurred since my last update in January 2022, and the situation is subject to change. For the most current information, consulting recent sources is recommended.

The impact of corruption and governance issues on businesses, particularly in the context of inadequate infrastructure, can be substantial and multifaceted. The challenges posed by corruption and governance deficiencies have repercussions on the overall business environment, affecting investor confidence, long-term planning, and expansion efforts. Here are some key ways in which corruption and governance issues impact businesses:

1. Investor Confidence:

- **Challenge:** Corruption erodes investor confidence. When businesses perceive that corruption is widespread, they may view the investment environment as unpredictable and risky.
- **Impact:** Reduced investor confidence can lead to a reluctance to commit significant capital to long-term projects. Investors may opt for safer, less-corrupt environments, limiting the inflow of foreign direct investment (FDI).

2. Risk Assessment:

- **Challenge:** Corruption and weak governance introduce uncertainties that make it challenging for businesses to conduct accurate risk assessments.

- **Impact:** Businesses may struggle to accurately gauge the risks associated with operating in a corrupt environment. This uncertainty can affect strategic decision-making and planning.

3. Long-Term Planning Hindered:

- **Challenge:** Corruption and governance deficiencies often contribute to a lack of stability and predictability in the business environment.
- **Impact:** Businesses find it difficult to engage in effective long-term planning. The absence of a stable and predictable environment hinders strategic decision-making and can lead to short-term, reactive business strategies.

4. Reduced Competitiveness:

- **Challenge:** Corruption can distort competition and favor businesses with close ties to corrupt practices. This can create an uneven playing field.
- **Impact:** Legitimate businesses that refuse to engage in corrupt practices may find it challenging to compete with less scrupulous competitors. This reduces overall competitiveness in the market.

5. Increased Operating Costs:

- **Challenge:** Corruption can lead to additional costs for businesses. Bribes or facilitation payments may be required to navigate bureaucratic obstacles.

- **Impact:** Increased operating costs diminish profit margins and hinder a company's ability to invest in innovation, expansion, or employee development.

6. Hindered Infrastructure Development:

- **Challenge:** Corruption and weak governance often lead to inadequate infrastructure development. Funds that should be allocated for infrastructure projects may be diverted.

- **Impact:** The lack of reliable infrastructure, such as transportation and energy networks, can hinder businesses' efficiency and increase operational costs. This, in turn, affects their ability to expand and compete effectively.

7. Challenges in Expansion Efforts:

- **Challenge:** Corruption can create obstacles to business expansion. Obtaining permits, licenses, or approvals may involve corrupt practices or face unnecessary delays.

- **Impact:** The difficulties in navigating corrupt systems may deter businesses from pursuing expansion plans. This can limit job creation and economic growth.

8. Vulnerability to Extortion:

- **Challenge:** Businesses operating in environments with corruption may be vulnerable to extortion and demands for bribes.
- **Impact:** The risk of extortion creates an unpredictable operating environment. Businesses may divert resources towards managing such risks rather than focusing on growth and innovation.

9. Reputational Risks:

- **Challenge:** Operating in a corrupt environment may expose businesses to reputational risks, especially if they are perceived as complicit in corrupt practices.
- **Impact:** Reputational damage can have long-term consequences, affecting customer trust, employee morale, and relationships with partners and stakeholders.

10. Limited Access to Finance:

- **Challenge:** Corruption can extend to financial institutions, affecting access to finance for businesses that refuse to engage in corrupt practices.
- **Impact:** Limited access to finance constraints businesses' ability to invest in capital-intensive projects, hindering growth and expansion plans.

To address these challenges, a concerted effort is needed to combat corruption, strengthen governance frameworks, and foster an environment conducive to ethical business practices. This involves collaboration between the government, private sector, and civil society to promote transparency, accountability, and the rule of law.

Examination of controversies, including corruption allegations, and their impact on economic development.

Controversies, particularly those involving corruption allegations, can have a profound impact on economic development. These controversies often create a ripple effect that extends beyond immediate concerns, affecting investor confidence, government credibility, and the overall business environment. Examining the step-by-step impact of controversies on economic development involves considering various aspects:

1. Initial Allegations and Investigations:

- **Start of Controversy:** Controversies typically begin with allegations of corruption or other malpractices within government or private entities. Investigations may be initiated to assess the veracity of the claims.

- **Impact:** The initial phase can introduce uncertainty as investors and businesses await the outcome of investigations. This uncertainty may lead to a cautious approach in decision-making, affecting investment plans.

2. Public Perception and Confidence:

- **Emergence of Scandal:** As details of the controversy unfold, public perception plays a crucial role. If corruption is substantiated, it can erode public trust in both the implicated entities and the broader economic system.

- **Impact:** A loss of public confidence can lead to social unrest, protests, and demands for accountability. This public sentiment may prompt businesses to reconsider their operations and investments.

3. Policy Uncertainty and Reforms:

- **Government Response:** Controversies often prompt governments to respond with policy changes, anti-corruption measures, or institutional reforms to address the root causes.

- **Impact:** While reforms are essential for long-term economic health, the uncertainty surrounding policy changes can create challenges for businesses adapting to new regulations. Investors may adopt a wait-and-see approach.

4. Market Reactions and Investor Flight:

- **Impact on Stock Markets:** Publicly traded companies implicated in controversies may experience declines in their stock values. Investors may sell off shares, leading to market volatility.

- **Impact:** Investor flight can have a cascading effect on the broader economy. The depreciation of stock values affects pension funds and individual investors, leading to a reduction in overall wealth and spending.

5. Credit Rating Downgrades:

- **International Perception:** Controversies can impact a country's international standing, affecting credit ratings. Downgrades may result in higher borrowing costs for the government and private sector.

- **Impact:** Elevated borrowing costs can impede infrastructure projects and government initiatives, hindering economic development. Businesses may face challenges in accessing affordable credit for expansion.

6. Impact on Foreign Direct Investment (FDI):

- **Global Investor Sentiment:** Widespread controversies can deter foreign investors, particularly if corruption is perceived as systemic. Global investors may opt for more stable markets.

- **Impact:** Reduced FDI limits capital inflow, hindering economic growth. Businesses reliant on foreign investment may struggle to secure the necessary funds for expansion and innovation.

7. Operational Disruptions and Economic Slowdown:

- **Business Disruptions:** Companies implicated in controversies may face legal challenges, operational disruptions, and reputational damage. This can impact their ability to contribute to economic activity.

- **Impact:** Operational disruptions can lead to a slowdown in economic activities. Businesses may delay or scale back expansion plans, affecting job creation and overall productivity.

8. Long-Term Repercussions and Rebuilding Trust:

- **Rebuilding Trust:** Addressing controversies requires sustained efforts to rebuild trust. Implementing anti-corruption measures and transparent governance practices are crucial for restoring confidence.
- **Impact:** The process of rebuilding trust is gradual. However, successful efforts can lead to renewed investor confidence, economic stability, and the potential for sustainable development.

9. Lessons Learned and Future Resilience:

- **Policy Adjustments:** Governments and businesses may learn from controversies and implement measures to enhance resilience against corruption. This can include strengthening institutions, improving transparency, and fostering a culture of accountability.
- **Impact:** While controversies initially pose challenges, they can serve as catalysts for positive change. Implementing lessons learned contributes to a more robust economic environment in the long run.

. **Allegations and Initial Investigation:**

- **Start of Controversy:** Controversies often commence with whistleblowers, media reports, or official disclosures raising allegations of corruption or malpractices. These claims may involve government officials or private entities.
- **Impact:** The exposure of alleged wrongdoing prompts public attention and scrutiny. The initiation of investigations is a crucial step toward determining the validity of the claims and holding those responsible accountable.

2. Transparency in Investigations:

- **Government Response:** A constructive response from the government involves transparent and impartial investigations. Establishing independent inquiry commissions or collaborating with external investigative bodies enhances credibility.
- **Impact:** Transparency in investigations demonstrates a commitment to accountability. It helps build public trust and sets the stage for constructive actions to address corruption at its roots.

3. Legal Proceedings and Judicial Independence:

- **Legal Scrutiny:** If the allegations are substantiated, legal proceedings should follow. Ensuring judicial independence is critical for a fair and impartial trial that upholds the rule of law.

- **Impact:** A fair legal process reinforces confidence in the justice system. It sends a signal that the legal framework is robust enough to address corruption and malpractices, fostering an environment of accountability.

4. Public Awareness and Engagement:

- **Communication Strategy:** Governments and entities involved should communicate openly with the public. Regular updates on the progress of investigations, legal proceedings, and corrective actions demonstrate a commitment to transparency.

- **Impact:** Public awareness and engagement empower citizens. Informed citizens can play an active role in demanding accountability and participating in the development of solutions to prevent future corruption.

5. Anti-Corruption Reforms:

- **Policy Response:** As investigations unfold, governments should enact and implement anti-corruption reforms. This may involve strengthening anti-corruption laws, enhancing oversight mechanisms, and promoting a culture of integrity.

- **Impact:** Policy responses signal a commitment to constructive change. Enacted reforms contribute to the development of a resilient framework that discourages corruption and promotes sustainable development.

6. Cooperation with International Bodies:

- **Global Collaboration:** In cases involving transnational corruption, cooperation with international bodies and agencies, such as the United Nations and Interpol, is constructive. Sharing information and collaborating on investigations reinforce global efforts against corruption.

- **Impact:** International collaboration enhances the effectiveness of anti-corruption measures. It contributes to the development of a global environment where corruption is actively combated, benefiting economic development on a broader scale.

7. Corporate Responsibility and Accountability:

- **Private Sector Engagement:** Private entities implicated in controversies should take responsibility. Implementing internal reforms, conducting independent audits, and holding individuals accountable for their actions are constructive steps.

- **Impact:** Corporate responsibility contributes to rebuilding trust. It sets an example for ethical business practices, positively influencing the overall business environment and fostering economic development.

8. Restitution and Asset Recovery:

- **Recovery Measures:** Where corruption results in financial losses, efforts should be made to recover misappropriated assets. Restitution and asset recovery mechanisms contribute to the restoration of public resources.

- **Impact:** The recovery of misappropriated funds directly benefits economic development. These resources can be redirected toward infrastructure projects, social programs, and other initiatives that contribute to national growth.

9. Educational Initiatives and Ethical Training:

- **Preventive Measures:** Governments and entities can implement educational initiatives to promote ethical behavior and integrity. Training programs on ethics and compliance foster a culture that prevents corruption.

- **Impact:** Preventive measures are constructive for long-term development. By instilling ethical values, future generations are better equipped to contribute to a transparent and accountable society.

10. Monitoring and Evaluation:

- **Ongoing Oversight:** Establishing mechanisms for ongoing monitoring and evaluation ensures the sustainability of reforms. Regular assessments help identify areas for improvement and reinforce a culture of accountability.
- **Impact:** Continuous oversight contributes to the consolidation of a transparent and accountable governance system. It ensures that lessons learned from controversies are integrated into institutional practices, fostering constructive and sustainable development over time.

Conclusion:

Controversies, especially those involving corruption allegations, have multifaceted and lasting impacts on economic development. The step-by-step examination highlights the interconnected nature of these effects, emphasizing the importance of addressing governance challenges promptly and implementing reforms to build a foundation for sustained economic growth. A commitment to transparency, accountability, and ethical practices is essential for fostering a conducive environment for businesses, investors, and the broader society.

Analysis of adaptive measures taken in response to economic crises. Adaptive measures in response to economic crises involve a combination of problem-solving strategies, creative thinking, and policy interventions aimed at stabilizing economies, mitigating negative impacts, and fostering recovery. Let's analyze some key adaptive measures taken in response to economic crises:

1. Fiscal Policy Adjustments:

- **Problem-Solving:** Governments often implement counter-cyclical fiscal policies, such as stimulus packages and tax adjustments, to address economic downturns. These measures aim to boost demand, support businesses, and protect vulnerable populations.

- **Creativity:** Creative fiscal policy responses may include targeted financial assistance to specific sectors heavily impacted by the crisis, innovative tax incentives, or public investment projects that create jobs and stimulate economic activity.

2. Monetary Policy Interventions:

- **Problem-Solving:** Central banks implement monetary policy measures, such as interest rate adjustments and quantitative easing, to manage liquidity, stabilize financial markets, and encourage borrowing and spending.

- **Creativity:** Creative monetary policy responses may involve unconventional measures, such as forward guidance, to provide clarity on future policy intentions and unconventional asset purchases to address specific challenges in financial markets.

3. Social Safety Nets and Welfare Programs:

- **Problem-Solving:** Governments enhance social safety nets to protect vulnerable populations from the economic impacts of a crisis. This includes expanded unemployment benefits, food assistance, and healthcare support.

- **Creativity:** Creative solutions may involve the rapid deployment of digital platforms for the disbursement of financial aid, targeted assistance for gig economy workers, and partnerships with private sector entities to ensure efficient delivery of support.

4. Debt Relief and Restructuring:

- **Problem-Solving:** Countries facing debt challenges may negotiate debt relief or restructuring agreements with creditors to ease financial burdens and create fiscal space for essential spending.

- **Creativity:** Creative approaches may involve the development of innovative financial instruments, such as GDP-linked bonds, which tie debt repayments to a country's economic performance, providing flexibility during times of crisis.

5. Innovative Economic Stimulus Programs:

- **Problem-Solving:** Governments design economic stimulus programs to spur economic activity. This can include infrastructure projects, green investments, and incentives for research and development.

- **Creativity:** Creative stimulus measures may involve "green recovery" initiatives that simultaneously address economic challenges and environmental concerns, fostering a sustainable and resilient recovery.

6. Digital Transformation and E-Commerce Support:

- **Problem-Solving:** The promotion of digital transformation and e-commerce becomes crucial during economic crises, facilitating business continuity, remote work, and online transactions.

- **Creativity:** Creative solutions involve providing training programs for businesses to adapt to digital platforms, supporting the development of local e-commerce ecosystems, and fostering innovation in digital services.

7. Labor Market Adaptations:

- **Problem-Solving:** Governments implement measures to address unemployment, such as job training programs, re-skilling initiatives, and support for industries experiencing growth.
- **Creativity:** Creative approaches may include public-private partnerships for workforce development, incentivizing businesses to hire through targeted subsidies, and creating platforms that connect job seekers with emerging opportunities.

8. International Collaboration and Coordination:

- **Problem-Solving:** Countries collaborate on a global scale to address shared challenges, such as through coordinated fiscal and monetary policies, debt relief initiatives, and international financial support.
- **Creativity:** Creative international collaboration involves the exploration of new frameworks for global economic governance,

innovative financing mechanisms for development, and the sharing of best practices in crisis response.

9. Green and Sustainable Investments:

- **Problem-Solving:** Governments recognize the opportunity to align economic recovery with sustainability goals, investing in green infrastructure, renewable energy, and environmentally conscious projects.
- **Creativity:** Creative solutions include the development of sustainable finance mechanisms, incentivizing businesses to adopt eco-friendly practices, and supporting research and innovation in green technologies.

10. Community Engagement and Grassroots Initiatives:

- **Problem-Solving:** Engaging communities and supporting grassroots initiatives are critical for addressing localized challenges and ensuring an inclusive recovery.
- **Creativity:** Creative community-based solutions involve leveraging local resources, supporting small businesses through community-driven programs, and fostering a sense of collective responsibility for economic resilience.

In summary, adaptive measures in response to economic crises require a combination of problem-solving skills and creative thinking. Policymakers, businesses, and communities must explore innovative strategies to address the unique challenges posed by each crisis, fostering resilience and contributing to sustainable economic development.

Conclusion:

As of my last knowledge update in January 2022, "Biyaism" is not a widely recognized term or concept. However, if you are referring to the leadership style or policies associated with Paul Biya, the long-serving President of

Cameroon, I can provide a conclusion based on general knowledge up to that point.

Biya's Leadership Style and Legacy:

Authoritarian Governance:

- Paul Biya has been in power since 1982 and is associated with a centralized and authoritarian style of governance. This longevity has both supporters commending stability and critics highlighting concerns about democratic principles.

Political Stability Amid Challenges:

- Biya's administration has maintained relative political stability in Cameroon, despite facing challenges such as regional tensions, economic struggles, and security issues, particularly in regions like Anglophone Cameroon.

Economic Development Efforts:

- Biya has overseen various economic development initiatives, but the results have been mixed. Challenges like corruption, infrastructural deficits, and socio-economic inequalities persist.

Values for Developing Strategies:

Inclusive Governance:

- Prioritize inclusivity in governance, ensuring representation from diverse regions, ethnicities, and social groups. Inclusive policies can contribute to social cohesion and stability.

Anti-Corruption Measures:

- Implement robust anti-corruption measures to enhance transparency and accountability. This can attract foreign investments, foster economic growth, and address concerns about mismanagement.

Investment in Education and Innovation:

- Prioritize education and innovation to build a skilled workforce and promote technological advancements. Investing in human capital is crucial for long-term economic development.

Infrastructure Development:

- Strategically invest in infrastructure projects to address transportation, energy, and communication challenges. Improved infrastructure can stimulate economic activities and attract investments.

Regional Cooperation:

- Foster regional cooperation and diplomatic ties to address cross-border challenges, promote trade, and strengthen collective efforts for regional development.

Environmental Sustainability:

- Embrace sustainable development practices to address environmental concerns. Green initiatives can contribute to global sustainability goals and attract international support.

Social Welfare Programs:

- Implement social welfare programs to address poverty, healthcare, and social inequalities. A focus on the well-being of citizens can contribute to stability and social harmony.

Human Rights Protections:

- Uphold human rights protections and ensure the rule of law. Respecting fundamental rights builds trust, both domestically and internationally, and contributes to a positive global image.

Concluding Thoughts:

The success of strategies for the development of Cameroon and other nations in Africa depends on a comprehensive and inclusive approach. Effective governance, economic reforms, and social investments must go hand in hand to address the diverse challenges these nations face.

Additionally, a commitment to democratic principles, respect for human rights, and cooperation on the regional and international stages can contribute to sustained development and progress. It's essential for leaders to engage with diverse perspectives, adapt to changing circumstances, and remain responsive to the needs of their populations for a more prosperous and inclusive future.